For those that like a little inspiration in their day…

COFFEE TABLE INSPIRATION
compiled by Donna Chisholm

My sincerest gratitude to the following for allowing me to use their quotations

QUOTES BY DR. JOHN DEMARTINI AND ATHENA STARWOMAN, with permission from Dr. John DeMartini
www.drdemartini.info

QUOTES BY ALBERT EINSTEIN, with permission from Albert Einstein Archives, Hebrew University of Jerusalem
www.alberteinstein.info

Source of quotes in order of appearance:
PAGE 10
An inscription in album of Adriana Enriques, the young daughter of an Italian colleague, dated October 1921; item number 9-247
PAGE 32
From an interview recorded by G.S. Viereck, published in Saturday Evening Post, 26 October 1929
PAGE 40
Written for one of Isaac Newton's anniversaries between 1927 and 1942. Item number 31-047
PAGE 44
From an interview recorded by G.S. Viereck, published in Saturday Evening Post, 26 October 1929
PAGE 60
Statement on behalf of Bertrand Russell, first published in the New York Times, 19 March 1940
PAGE 80
From The World As I See It, originally published in Forum and Century, 1930

QUOTES BY NAPOLEON HILL, with permission of the Napoleon Hill Foundation www.naphill.org

QUOTES BY ROWENA SZESZERAN-MCEVOY, with permission from Rowena Szeszeran-McEvoy
www.maxfitnesscollege.com

Photography:
All space photos have been sourced from the National Aeronautics and Space Administration (NASA) web site.
You can visit http://grin.hq.nasa.gov
FIREWORKS, PAGE 37
© Interlighttv|Dreamstime.com – www.dreamstime.com/Interlighttv_info
BEE, PAGE 79
© Violetta Honkisz|Dreamstime.com – www.dreamstime.com/Atteloi_info
All other photos belong to Steve Van Aperen. If you like his photos, please visit www.redbubble.com and search for stevepolygraph

Your greatest challenge in life will be to stand at the meeting of the two eternities, to stand in the present moment, in the now between the past and future eternities

—DR. JOHN F. DEMARTINI

To those who believe no proof is necessary, to those who don't no proof is possible.
Waste no words on those who seek not

—ATHENA STARWOMAN 1945-2004

The pursuit of truth and beauty is a sphere of activity in which we are permitted to remain children all our lives

—ALBERT EINSTEIN 1879-1955

Worry not about the opinions of others

—EPICTETUS C. 50-120AD

Nature and wisdom never are at strife

—PLUTARCH C. 46-120AD

The soul never thinks without a picture

—ARISTOTLE 384-322BC

Astronomy compels the soul to look upwards and leads us from this world to another

—PLATO C. 424-348BC

Obstacles are those frightful things you see when you take your eyes off the goal

—HENRY FORD 1863-1947

You can regret the chances you didn't take…. Or, you can remember the fun you had and the lessons you learnt by taking them!!

—ROWENA SZESZERAN-MCEVOY

Madison Ave

st 42nd St

Step up to the plate and say "I can" - nobody else can do it for you

—DONNA CHISHOLM

Never discourage anyone who continually makes progress, no matter how slow

—ARISTOTLE 384-322BC

If you must speak ill of another, do not speak it, write it in the sand near the water's edge

—NAPOLEON HILL 1883-1970

Man, alone, has the power to transform his thoughts into physical reality; man, alone, can dream and make his dreams come true

—NAPOLEON HILL 1883-1970

Imagination is more important than knowledge. Knowledge is limited.
Imagination encircles the world

—ALBERT EINSTEIN 1879-1955

Whatever limits us we call fate

—RALPH WALDO EMERSON 1803-1882

Be a bright spark in someone else's day

—DONNA CHISHOLM

The greatest achievement was at first and for a time, a dream.
Dreams are the seedlings of reality.

—JAMES ALLEN 1864-1912

Watch the stars, and from them learn. To the Master's honor all must turn, each in its track, without a sound, forever tracing Newton's ground (written by Albert Einstein about Isaac Newton)

—ALBERT EINSTEIN 1879-1955

Take a deep breath, and then do it anyway!

—DONNA CHISHOLM

The human mind, no matter how highly trained, cannot grasp the Universe. We are in the position of a little child entering a huge library whose walls are covered to the ceilings with books in many different tongues. The child knows that someone must have written these books. It does not know who or how. It does not understand the languages in which they are written. But the child notes a definite plan in the arrangement of the books - a mysterious order which it does not comprehend, but only dimly suspects

—ALBERT EINSTEIN 1879-1955

Silence is one of the great arts of conversation

—CICERO 106-46BC

When was the last time you had fun like a child and laughed without hesitation?

—ROWENA SZESZERAN-MCEVOY

Years may wrinkle the skin, but to give up enthusiasm wrinkles the soul

—SAMUEL ULLMAN 1840-1924

Listen to your inner voice. It starts with a whisper,
but the more you listen, the louder it gets

—DONNA CHISHOLM

Most people never run far enough on their first wind to find out they've got a second. Give your dreams all you've got and you'll be amazed at the energy that comes out of you

—WILLIAM JAMES 1842-1910

We are what we repeatedly do. Excellence, therefore, is not an act but a habit

—ARISTOTLE 384-322BC

Your outer world is but a reflection of your inner world

—DR. JOHN F. DEMARTINI

Great spirits have always encountered violent opposition from mediocre minds

—ALBERT EINSTEIN 1879-1955

Stop being a moon. Stop living by reflected light. Get into action and convert yourself into a living sun. You can do it

—WILLIAM WALKER ATKINSON 1862-1932

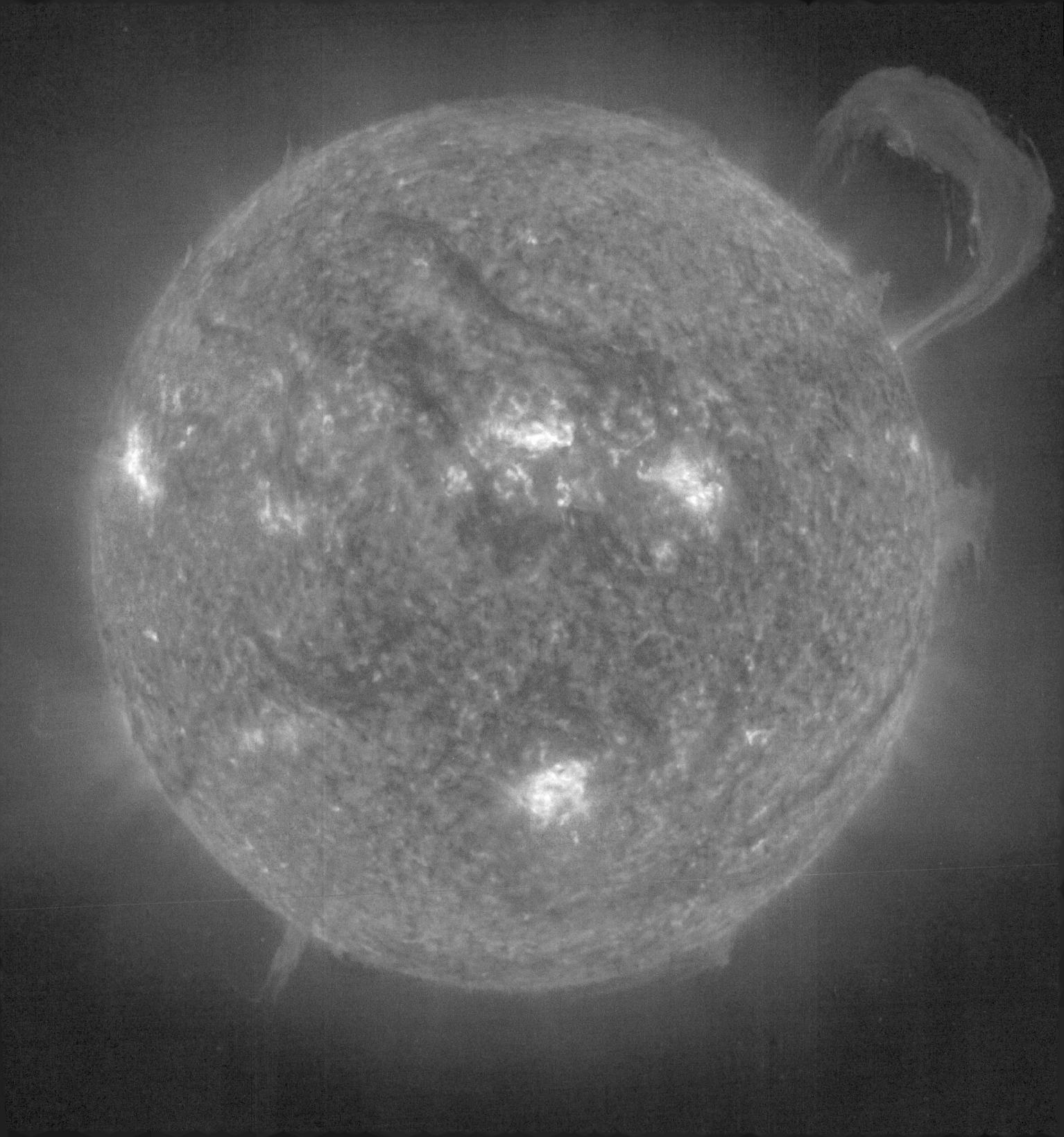

Self-control is strength. Right thought is mastery. Calmness is power

—JAMES ALLEN 1864-1912

Shine like gold, sparkle like a diamond, let the hidden gem in you be seen by the world!

—DONNA CHISHOLM

The high-minded man must care more for the truth than for what people think

—ARISTOTLE 384-322BC

Let us not look back in anger nor forward in fear but around us in awareness

—LELAND VAL VANDEWALL

Cherish your visions and your dreams as they are the children of your soul,
the blueprints of your ultimate achievements

—NAPOLEON HILL 1883-1970

Everything in the universe goes by indirection. There are no straight lines

—RALPH WALDO EMERSON 1803-1882

You are worthy. You are loved. I believe in you

—DONNA CHISHOLM

Every efficient act is a success in itself, and if every act in your life is an efficient one, your whole life MUST be a success

—WALLACE D. WATTLES 1860-1911

The most beautiful thing we can experience is the mysterious.
It is the fundamental emotion which stands at the cradle of true art and true science

—ALBERT EINSTEIN

Too low they build, who build beneath the stars

—EDWARD YOUNG 1681-1765

Shine in your own magnificence

—DONNA CHISHOLM

Don't wait until later, you only have now

—DONNA CHISHOLM

Success is the good fortune that comes from aspiration, desperation, perspiration and inspiration

—EVAN ESAR 1899-1995

You don't have to BECOME a star, you ARE a star already!

—DONNA CHISHOLM

Be inspired. Live with love. Recognise your own magnificence. Live your life

—DONNA CHISHOLM

www.coffeetableinspiration.com

Cover Design and Book Design by

Glen M. Edelstein
HUDSON VALLEY DESIGN
134 Sierra Vista Lane
Valley Cottage, NY 10989 USA
glenede@gmail.com
1.845.642.3352